The Less-Stressing Way of Educating Your Children

Impossibly Simple Tips of Disciplining Children without Shouting or Spanking

By: Ruth Hill

9781635014341

D1806551

Publishers Notes

Disclaimer – Speedy Publishing LLC

Speedy Publishing LLC

40 E Main Street, Newark, Delaware, 19711

Contact Us: 1-888-248-4521

Website: http://www.speedypublishing.co

REPRINTED Paperback Edition: 9781635014341:

Manufactured in the United States of America

DEDICATION

This book is dedicated to Benny. I must have done something right in my past life to be blessed with a wonderful partner.

TABLE OF CONTENTS

Chapter 1- Dealing with the Children of the Modern Age

Television today is still a "baby sitter" both for adults and preschoolers. When people are bored or simply want to rest, they watch TV. Some are not really interested to watch at all. They need the TV to put them to sleep. As soon as you turn it off, they wake up. With the remote control, watching TV can be a dizzying experience. I get confused with what characters go with what plot. What with that mysterious hand switching channels during commercial breaks, you find yourself following several shows at the same time. Sometimes you have to shout, "Stop!" and confiscate the remote control. "Please decide which program you want and stick to it". That was supposed to be final but what's this switching channel again? "Mom, there are commercial breaks!" would be the excuse.

Today's TV imports still have family-oriented shows and the rest are soap operas, game shows and their local counterparts which include slapsticks or tearjerkers, noontime variety shows, movie personalities' song and dance, and movie Dom's gossip sessions.

The Less-Stressing Way of Educating Your Children

These are the kinds of shows very young children are exposed to. Most of these are shown at times when kids are awake and those of school age are already home.

Programming leaves much to be desired. One of the positive developments in local TV is the emergence of talk shows discussing current issues as well as TV-magazine formats. For mothers, "Sesame Street" is heaven-sent. You can put the little tykes in front of the TV (at least 4 "rulers" away – instructions to the little ones) and have a little break from mothering. But violence even in cartoons is the order of the day. You see Bugs Bunny hammered on the head or blown to pieces by Sam his Enemy No. 1 or Road Runner running over the coyote. Tom and Jerry and now their sons slug it out; and of course, the Japanese robots and the superheroes in the endless fight between good and evil. You don't have to think about the violent "drama" teleplays or movies and their trailers, especially the one where the lead actress pokes a gun on the actor's head who says, "Go ahead, and shoot it". You'd probably close your eyes and shudder to think of the countless kids exposed to this kind of violence. And you parents are helpless. Ads just pop out of the boob tube every 15 minutes and you can't tell which one will go on. Not unless the stations publish a list of advertisers or sponsors. Boy! That's going to be a long list!

The crucial thing about TV is it is a powerful medium. Repetitious subliminal messages are being exploited by advertisements that target kids. They are mesmerized by commercials. Cigarette and liquor ads suggest, "It is good to smoke and drink" without warning about its dangers. They often show images of sophisticated living.

Teachers reveal their frustration with college students who have limited concentration that usually lasts only for 15 minutes due to commercial gap syndrome. They suffer from what noted psychologists term "attention deficit disorder". Moreover, these teachers lament. Kids raised by TV hardly read, preconditioned as they are by TV-spoon feeding. (How many students actually read a book for their term paper? If they do, they choose a very short book but most just rent a DVD version.) There is nothing wrong with this audiovisual education like "The Planet Earth" but reading is entirely different from watching.

Reading develops the imagination unlike TV, where the camera can focus on the smallest detail. The fast pacing of images gives the illusion that "life is never continuous...it is fragmentized; it is made up of commercial breaks. And if one doesn't like what is seen and heard, one can change channels". In reality, one can "change channels" in one's mind and switch to fantasy.

Television's powerful medium can be utilized in a positive way. Already public service ads by both the station and advertiser are being shown. It aims to educate the public on traffic and safety rules. Effective communication must be two-way. TV programs now feature citizens' woes and call the attention of the concerned government agency or ask citizens' cooperation in government programs. Not surprisingly, this produces faster results. It is hoped that the government will subsidize alternative TV productions that will really give wholesome entertainment, education and develop local talent rather than the superstar "mentality" and its subsequent commercial rating that dominates the industry today.

In the high-tech world of communications via satellites, fax and computers, our children are bombarded with instant, varied and conflicting messages. It is easy to be carried away with images of fun and make-believe like the MTVs that seem to be getting more and more hallucinatory and lead an aimless life. Or children of the TV generation might be indecisive due to the myriad choices they are confronted with. This is real life. There is no instant replay or fast-forward. "Changing channels" needs a lot of thinking and weighing of consequences, advantages and disadvantages. There is great pressure not to be traditional. Don't apologize. You can still be progressive and choose traditional values. Indeed, your children need to have an anchor and a focus – good old-fashioned principles and priorities.

How and Why Children Grow in a Culture of Violence

Like most of the parents, you are probably against guns. At the mere sight of them, your knees turn to jelly. A gun-less society is ideal but only law-abiding citizens can make it one. If only the goons use guns, who will protect the gun-less citizens? Nowadays, it's hard to tell who are the law enforcers and the law-breakers. You must be able to enforce "toys for peace" in your home. You should be conscious about this, as your boys and girls graduate from plastic toys that go "bang! Bang!" to water guns. What are popular now are air soft guns using plastic pellets. They are quite expensive. This is probably one step ahead of video or role-playing games, where one uses the computer or imagination. In war games, they can act it out.

You probably don't notice it but when your kids start playing war games, their relationship skills improve. They become a team with a hobby to share. It's good, clean fun. Nobody gets hurt. They wear protective goggles or face masks, long sleeves and long pants. (It seems there are some adults who join, not to play, but to hurt.) The children's justifications should never change your stand about toy guns. They know they can never ask you to buy such guns for them. (So they'd probably try asking their other parent.) Besides, you reaction is always economic: "How much? That's a month's groceries! No way!"

But when violence is deliberate, such as in hazing, then that's a different story. This is no longer a game. The pain is real. It is not like those "blood pellets" you can wipe away when the game is over. You can actually have blood on your hands. Hazing does not teach brotherhood. It teaches revenge. So this batch was made to take a gulp of milk, spit it out, and pass the same glass down the line. From a half-filled glass, by the time it gets to the last guy, it's nearly full. Next year, this same batch will do the same, or worse, to their neophytes. And so the violence escalates. Is this a rite of passage every boy must undergo to be a man, or a girl to be a woman? A father, especially one who got by without joining any fraternity, is proof enough that fraternities are not necessary. If by brotherhood, it means cheating by test paper leaks and connections, then you shouldn't want that for your children.

They say the culture of violence is bred by violence in comics, movies and television. That enough exposure to violence can dull one's sense and one can become insensitive to gore and blood. Power can be such a heady experience. Guns or even a car can give one a feeling of power. You've seen houseboys transformed into veritable kings of the road, once they get behind the steering wheel. Can you imagine those out of school youth recruited to be security guards and issued guns? What can we do about this culture of violence? Parents ask the schools to be stricter with those involved in frat violence. For students, the best thing is to boycott fraternities. Those who join are mostly insecure students from the province who really need some form of brotherhood, as they are new in the city or university. They do not know that one can pass the course and find jobs based on one's merits.

Fratmen are popular with girls. Well, girls, frat membership does not make a man – especially when the measure is whether one can stand a beating and be able to beat up others in turn. Fraternities will eventually die if there will be no new recruits. Aside from limiting your children's exposure to violence in mass media, you have to teach them how to handle power. With power come greater responsibilities. Being a true leader means humility and service, not giving orders to slaves. Moreover, fellowship can be achieved without undergoing or inflicting pain. You can't completely protect your children from violence since it exists in their environment. The most you could do is to arm your children with values so that, in time, when they encounter violence, they will know what to do and hopefully make the right decision.

CHAPTER 2- BECOMING AN EFFECTIVE PARENT THROUGH POSITIVE ENCOURAGEMENT

Encouraging the Young to be Successful

What kind of parent are you – an encourager or an intimidator? The encourager stresses working towards a certain goal. The intimidator stresses winning. For this kind of parent, "It's the results that count... not the effort, not the intentions." And what results! Useless deaths.

You have heard about graduating college students resorting to suicide for not graduating with honors in a family of medalists or in another case, for failing to graduate at all. Those who choose to live become obsessive about reaching the top, even at the expense of others. Some are immobilized – afraid to try unless success is guaranteed. Naturally, the one encouraged first is happy about the praises heaped on him or her. But when you give your child the opposite, the reactions would be: disbelief, anger...and later, self-doubt. Somehow, all those discouraging comments get to you.

That exercise made us step back and examine the atmosphere you create at home. Is it encouraging or downgrading? Are you an encourager or an intimidator? Note that your targets are parent-volunteers, so they were aware that this was some sort of exercise, yet it affected their self-esteem. Imagine how a string of negative messages or put-downs can affect an insecure child? Encouragement is not the same as pampering though. Pampering means regularly doing something the teenagers can do for themselves such as fixing their room, preparing lunch, or even waking up. Overindulgence makes a child irresponsible. Overprotection makes kids dependent on others. Praising is not encouragement. Praise is a reward given for an achievement. It fosters competition and fear of failure. Encouragement is given for effort and improvement. It fosters cooperation and self-esteem. It inspires confidence and acceptance. Of course, you should give praise when it is due. But encouragement does not thrive on praises alone. A child can tell empty praises from real ones. Besides, there is danger that a child hungry for praise will merely conform to please and won't feel okay unless praised.

Encouragement means emphasis on strengths and assets, other than faults. It is non-judgmental - accepting the level of accomplishment of each child. Unrealistic expectations could be stressful to a child. If circumstances or physical inability prevents him or her from fulfilling certain expectations, then you can't say, "You can do it." The kid would be bound for certain disappointment. It's just like saying "It won't hurt" when an injection really hurts. You can't fool children. Sometimes, you have to help your children set realistic goals. When one of the kids wants to enter a contest, you're all out rooting for him or her – whether it's an art contest, a science contest, or whatever. Some kids start counting their prizes even before they submit their entries. In those cases, you explain the odds and make the project so much fun that it is the effort that counts.

Other discouraging family practices you learned at seminars are: permissiveness (which makes a child unconcerned about others' rights), inconsistent discipline (results in feeling that life is unfair) and denial of feelings. A person who is not in touch with his or her own feelings can never relate to others. "Poor you," mothers often say to a child after bumping his or her head. Sometimes, parents even go to such lengths as spanking the object that caused pain to appease the crying child. It's not funny. It's stupid. Pity breeds a discouraging family atmosphere. It does not help build confidence in the child. When your kids come to you for help, be glad. Don't "shoo" them away by lecturing:

• "Is this the best you can do?"

• "I don't want to see line of 7s or Cs."

• "With these grades, you don't deserve to go to school! Why should I spend thousands if you don't care to study? Do you still want to go to college or not?"

• "What's your ambition in life? To be a janitor?"

• "Don't ask stupid questions. Use your common sense."

• "You should know better."

The Less-Stressing Way of Educating Your Children

Most of these are recordings in your minds, handed down to you by your parents and their parents. It's about time you got out of that mode and reprogram yourself by consciously creating an encouraging environment at home. It is not the one-sided "Honor thy father and mother." Each family should work out their own "Treaty of Friendship, Cooperation and Security", with children given the opportunities to give opinions, participate in decisions, and take on responsibilities according to their capabilities. "Don't expect to change your teenager." The beginning of change is to accept one's mistakes. Saying sorry to your children can do wonders in bridging the generation gap. It is only human to let the children know, "Hey, kids! Parents need some encouragement too!

Using Positive Phrases, Not Bribery or Punishment

How do you discipline your child? Most of the parents would admit to having spanked their children at least once. In behavioral studies, 3 approaches to eliciting a desired behavior can also be found in parents' discipline styles: positive reinforcement, negative reinforcement, and punishment. Positive reinforcement entails providing an event (like a reward or praise) that increases the probability of the desired behavior being repeated. With negative reinforcement, a desired behavior is drawn out through the elimination of an adverse event (e.g. child learns to wake up earlier for school every day because getting caught in traffic makes him nauseous).

Punishment, often confused with negative reinforcement, involves increasing an adverse event to decrease or stop negative behavior. Child experts agree that, of the 3, positive reinforcement is the best way to draw out positive behavior in children and even keep negative behavior in check. Some parents mistakenly associate positive reinforcement with bribing or giving material rewards. In bribery, you promise something bigger and more valuable than the behavior you are expecting. You also tend to negotiate or beg; even increasing the value of the prize, just to make sure that the behavior you wish is manifested.

Giving a child verbal encouragement or small tokens after they exhibit a certain desirable behavior does not qualify for bribery. Other parents steer clear from positive reinforcements for fear that they might spoil their child. However, it is far from spoiling if the reward given is commensurate to the positive behavior exhibited by the child. Material rewards need not be expensive things; small tokens like stickers or erasers are hardly decadent. Non-material reinforcements are highly recommended: a hug, a wink, and a compliment for a job well done. There is no specific age at which to start using positive reinforcement; children learn to relate reinforcements to their behavior after several similar experiences and patterns.

Good deeds that were reinforced at an early age become part of the child's personality. As children grow, their needs will differ in the same way that our expectations of them will expand. So, the reinforcements may change, but the general principle remains. The success of positive reinforcement greatly depends not on the child, but on the adult using it as a disciplinary approach. When used successfully, positive reinforcement can develop a child's intrinsic motivation. It can provide children some understanding of expectations and behavior.

Here are the main points to help parents effectively wield positive reinforcement:

•Select and define the deed.

Be clear on what is acceptable or unacceptable behavior at home. Provide observable, measurable progress by specifying which behavior you want the child to repeat. Refrain from giving abstract directives. Instead of "Behave while eating" say "Sit on your chair, do not play with your utensils, and tidy up your eating area after eating the food."

•Choose your reinforcements.

Reinforcers must be appropriate for – and as valuable as – the behavior. They should match the child's age, abilities, and the effort required to earn them. Kids have individual preferences. A reinforce that is not significant to your child will bear no value. For example, preschool children will like getting stickers and hugs, while teenagers may prefer getting an extended curfew.

•Timing is everything.

Consistency is the key. Make it routine for your children. It helps them internalize rules and expectations. Also, immediately reinforce good behavior. The shorter the delay between the behavior and reinforcer then the greater the chance of strengthening the behavior. When reinforcing a new skill, reinforce continuously. Once the behavior has been established in the child, then you can gradually delay and decrease reinforcements.

•Be diverse.

Varying reinforcements prevents satiation in a child. Use your imagination to come up with different reinforcements. Opt for assorted nonmaterial reinforcements. You will be surprised that not all kids want material things as reinforcements. Hugs, pats on the back, and words have equal, if not more, significance to them.

•Complement praise with encouragement.

Pairing reinforcements with words of praise and encouragement works best to retain or repeat a good behavior. Praise usually denotes the person, and some judgment is made on him or her. Encouragement is taking notice of the behavior or action, instead of the person. An example of praise is "You're a good girl" while "I like the way you helped the lady carry her bag," are words of encouragement.

By using words of praise and encouragement, it puts recognition and meaning to one's presence and work. Why Too Much Praise is Ineffective International studies have shown that praise definitely increases people's inner interest in activities. Anything too much or too little is proven ineffective. Too much praise is ineffective because it comes too easy and often reduces the value of praise. Too little of it and lack of consistency do not give it much significance, as well. Here are some keywords to remember when giving praise:

•Immediate. Praise kids right after the good behavior occurs. This way, they know instantly which behavior is reinforced.

•Specific. Say exactly which behavior, action, or words you liked. For example, "Thank you for putting your toys back in the bin," or "I like the way you shared your toys with your friends." If the action was partly wrong, focus only on the positive side.

•Frequent. Be consistent in saying words of praise every time kids do something good. Do not let any good or improved deed pass unnoticed. This reminds kids, positively, that a particular behavior should be part of their way of life.

- Sincere. Put emphasis on the feelings and values instead of judging kids as "good" or "bad". For example, if you see your child politely asking for his or her turn in playing a video game, say, "I like the way you asked your brother if you could play after him. I think that was a polite thing to do."

- Varied. Use different praise statements. Repeating the same thing may lose its impact and value. Changing it is also one way to increase kids' emotional vocabulary, which will help them express themselves as they grow.

When Do You Start Spoiling Your Child?

Spoiling a child takes time. It consists of a series of early life decisions and events which parents or guardians make for young children. The course of these early life decisions can eventually develop a child's preferences: his or her way of reacting toward individuals around him or her, study habits, eating habits, and social skills. Even before the child is ready, today's children have too many options. Moreover, due to work demands of harried parents, the resulting guilt about time for and with the child can be a potent recipe for spoiling.

Today's parent can opt to give in to tantrums and giving too many material things to keep the peace and assuage guilt. Likewise, there may be inconsistencies in the manner of dealing with the child among the adults. The result is a spoiled child. Take for example these two extreme cases.

The first is 10-year-old Chase who was unwilling to go to school and do any schoolwork if he were not to receive any compensation, like toys or electronic games. This young boy would force his will on his parents by banging his head on the wall repeatedly until his demands are met. Giving in to such demands is not the answer, as they most likely lead to only bigger, unrealistic, and self-centered demands.

Another case is 4-year-old Paul who was unable to appreciate his possessions, as he would be given new toys on almost a daily basis. When Paul's toy is broken, he would quickly ask, "Can we buy another one?"

Discipline is often associated with punishment. Actually, punishments and rewards are just aspects of it. Discipline, if applied consistently and with consideration of the child's level of understanding, is the best way of instilling a sense of responsibility in children like Chase and Paul. This starts with the parent being clear about what the child can and cannot do. Slowly, if the parents are clear and consistent, the child internalizes a moral compass to help guide him or her in decision-making.

In the case of Chase, there was inconsistency in the way the parents dealt with him. It was his mother who would set boundaries, like limiting the toys being bought and the amount of time he is allowed to play with his gaming unit. Chase's father, in an effort to spend quality time with his son, would inadvertently sabotage these rules by buying toys and allowing his son to play when they would spend time together.

Discipline is an ongoing process and cannot be done overnight. It requires constant compromise among parents and guardians attempting to instill it on their children. Other factors to take into consideration are family dynamics and personal values. These issues were very prominent in the case of Paul. Paul is the younger of two boys, both coming from different marriages. Paul's mother has difficulty spending time with her children, as she spends most of her time away from home. She also has a tendency to give in to Paul's demands in order for him to quiet down and refrain from throwing tantrums. It is never too late to instill discipline. Sit down with your significant other today and list down the areas that need to be addressed in the life of your child, as the effort you make today will shape the man or woman your child will be in the future.

CHAPTER 3- USING CHORES TO TEACH VALUES

Chores can help develop a sense of responsibility and self-worth in your child. It should be understood by all family members that chores are expected and necessary to a household running successfully and efficiently. They can help create a sense of unity and family and are a great way for your child to learn about teamwork. Parents should take special care to handle the delegation of chores to children so they don't become a source of frustration or create arguments.

Allow your child to have an active say in the delegation of chores. Give them choices. We all have household chores that we don't like to do, but if it's a chore the child enjoys doing, then there's less likelihood it will create a battle in the end. The child will most likely appreciate having the chance to be heard and having a choice.

It's imperative that you set parameters early on for the successful completion of a chore. They may not perform up to snuff when they first start performing the chore, but show them where improvement is needed and praise them for a strong effort. Also make sure the child understands there will be repercussions if they only put forth a minimal effort. Ensure that the child understands the need for the chore's effective and efficient completion. Set consequences for substandard completion as a team. Make sure they see that if they don't perform their chores, it affects the other members of the team. Spouses must work together and be a strong example for their children by completing their own chores each day. And don't allow a child to undermine your authority by battling with you over a designated chore. Stand your ground and don't give in, and emphasize the consequence and negative effect an uncompleted chore has on the family.

And keep an open mind when a child wants to discuss their thoughts or express their opinions about chores. Make sure the conversation stays positive and on target.

Track Accomplishments Using the Chore Chart

It can be very frustrating to ask your child over and over again to complete their chores without them ever getting done. If this describes your house to a tee, consider designing a chore chart. Chores might include taking out the garbage, doing the dishes, cleaning their room, yard work or putting laundry in the laundry room. Each chore has to be done just once or twice a week. Anything more is unrealistic. After your child completes each chore, they can put a check mark on the chore chart. At the end of each week, it's very inspiring for both parent and child to look at the chore chart and easily see that each designated job was completed. Just like us with our 'to do' lists, your child will find great satisfaction in being able to check off each chore as it is completed and take pride knowing they accomplished a set task or list of tasks.

Once you've sat down with your child and discussed and designed a chore chart, it's time to discuss the rewards for accomplishing each task listed. Perhaps at your home you decide you will give a set sum for each task accomplished. If you should decide to grant your child some sort of monetary allowance, make sure it's age appropriate and granted on a regular basis. A good rule of thumb is 50 cents per year of age. So your 8 year old child would earn $4.00 per week if each chore on the list has been completed. If it has not been, they do not receive their allowance.

This is a great opportunity for you to teach your children the value of both earning and saving money, and also giving back. Perhaps the child can divide their allowance into thirds: 1/3 to spend, 1/3 to save, and 1/3 to use to help those less fortunate than them. You might also want to consider designing a 'bank book' for each portion of the allowance and tuck each into three separate coffee cans or money jars, and that way you and your child will be able to keep track of how much has been saved, how much has been spent, and how much of their allowance has gone to help someone else.

Should you decide to use non-monetary incentives as chores payment, be sure you set clear parameters for your child. Be sure they understand that two hours each weekend of their favorite video game or going to see a movie with mom or dad is only earned by completing the chore list successfully each week. You might want to consider writing these on a slip of paper as 'currency' for the child to keep in their 'privilege bank' and they can cash it in with you when they'd like.

Regardless of the method you choose, keep in mind that this can be a valuable tool for both you and your child.

Why the Whining?

"Mooooooooooooom!"

It's irritating, it's frustrating and it gets on your last nerve. Though it's obnoxious and unacceptable, it's actually an effective way for your child to get your attention. It's whining. But, like other bad habits, you can nip it in the bud early on with a few simple strategies to teach your child there are other appropriate, effective forms of communicating with you.

First, try limiting the situations that trigger it. Avoid extra errands when the kids are hungry. Don't let them get involved in a frustrating game or project prior to bedtime. Pay attention when your child is talking, as sometimes whining is a reaction when a child feels you aren't giving them your full attention. Praise them for not whining and talking in a normal and understandable voice that allows you to fully understand what they are saying to you.

When the whining begins, don't overreact. Keep your response simple, calm and neutral. Ask your child to repeat the request in a normal tone. When giving in seems inevitable, don't delay. If you must finish the grocery shopping so you can put dinner on the table, for instance, and your child starts whining for a snack, offer something healthy right away.

Once a limit has been set, parents should follow through. It's imperative that both parents are on board with this limit and fully follow through when the whining rule has been violated.

If you have an older child that's developing a whining habit, suggest they come up with a solution to their perceived boredom or other voiced problem. If you suggest possible alternatives, it might just prolong the child's whining.

Sometimes whining can be the result of trauma and trouble in their life. A divorce, serious family illness or problems at school may be at the root. Additional positive attention and quality one-on-one time may be just the medicine your child needs at a time like this. Your pediatrician can also suggest alternatives to curb whining should the positive attention and disciplinary actions be ineffective.

CHAPTER 4- OF HABITS AND HOBBIES

Thumb sucking is a concern many parents have. Toddlers suck their thumbs because it's comforting and calming. It's probably something they did before they were born, and they revert back to it when they are nervous, agitated, scared or ill. They may also use it to lull themselves back to sleep in the middle of the night.

Parents shouldn't concern themselves unless it continues after the age their permanent teeth begin to appear, around six years old. Experts say that it's the intensity of the thumb sucking and the tongue's thrust that deforms teeth and makes braces necessary later. Children who rest their thumb passively in their mouth are less likely to have difficulty than children who suck aggressively. If you're concerned, closely monitor your child and analyze his or her technique. If they appear to be sucking vigorously, you may want to begin curbing the habit earlier.

Punishing or nagging your child to stop won't help, because it's usually an automatic response. Attempting to curb it by putting an elastic bandage on his or her thumb, or another such method, will seem like unjust punishment, especially since they indulge in the habit for comfort and security.

Try to wait it out. Children usually give up thumb sucking when they've found other ways to calm and comfort themselves. Consider offering them alternatives to comfort themselves with, such as a soft blanket or lullaby toy

The key is to notice when and where your child is likely to suck their thumb and offer an alternative. If it happens while they are tired, try giving more naps. If they suck their thumb frequently while watching television, try to distract them with a toy that will keep their hands occupied.

Older children may need gentle reminders to curtail thumb sucking while in public, and praise should be given freely when the child finds and uses an acceptable alternative. Your child's pediatric dentist can offer other suggestions for helping your child kick the thumb sucking habit.

Healthy Hobbies

Hobbies benefit children in many ways. They gives a child an opportunity to express themselves, discover themselves, and build self-esteem. They are also great educational tools. A child interested in rock collecting learns about geology and science, and a child in writing stories learns about sentence structure and proper grammar. Hobbies teach children to set and achieve goals, solve problems, and make decisions. They can also set the course for what your child becomes later in life, as they often turn into lifelong interests or careers.

Children who have hobbies are usually following in their parents footsteps, so set a good example by pursuing your own hobby.

Your child will need space for their hobby, so find an area designated specifically for the hobby so they can work on it. Realize that hobbies can sometimes be quite messy, so be at the ready for messes, as they come with the territory.

Be available to your child to provide guidance, support, and encouragement. This is a great time to teach your child strong work habits, such as following directions closely, setting goals, and proper planning and organization. Show them that nothing worthwhile is ever easy, especially when they begin to become frustrated with their progress. It's also a good time to teach them about personal responsibility and show them how important it is to properly care for their work area and their 'tools of the trade.'

Children will be more encouraged to work on their hobbies if activities like watching television or playing video games are limited. It's been noted by experts that by age 15, the average child has spent more time watching television than sitting in a classroom. Again, here's where setting a good example is crucial. Instead of watching that four-hour football game on Saturday, turn the TV off and work on your own hobby. Your child may want to join in or work on his or her own, as a result.

Hobbies are rewarding and enriching parts of our lives, so encourage your child to explore their own interests and find a hobby of their very own.

Stop with the Interruptions, Please

Trying to teach your child not to interrupt can sometimes be an exercise in frustration.

Telling them there's a time to interrupt (in case of a fire) and a time to not interrupt (boredom) isn't enough. Putting these principles into practice is easier said than done, especially for a very verbal or high-energy kid. That's why now is a good time to revisit some basic lessons about good manners and teaching your child to wait their turn to speak.

First of all, set a reasonable expectation. School-aged children have a difficult time holding their thoughts for more than a few minutes. Indicate to them as best as you can that you'll be with them as soon as possible and then stay true to your word.

Develop some ideas for them to occupy themselves with while you're on the phone or otherwise unavailable. Keep a box full of puzzles, crayons, colorful markers or other quiet toys nearby that they can only use when you have to make a call. Set snacks and drinks on an accessible level so they don't have to interrupt you for help.

When you need to make a call or have an important conversation with a visitor, head off trouble by saying you're about to phone someone or have a conversation and estimate how long you expect to talk. Ask them if they need anything before you make your call or have your conversation with your company. Then, do your best to adhere to that time schedule, and excuse yourself from the conversation long enough to check on them. Let them know you'll be a bit longer if that's the case and see if they need anything before returning to your conversation.

Reading is a great tool to teach manners. Find several books on the subject, and then read them together. Discuss afterwards what your child learned from the story and how they'll handle a similar situation in their life the next time it occurs.

And as always, children learn what they live. Your child is very unlikely to learn not to interrupt if they hear you, your spouse, or their siblings constantly interrupting each other. Your actions have a strong influence on your child, so be a good example. Ask permission to speak before speaking, and apologize when you inadvertently interrupt.

Potty Training

Your child is showing all the signs of being ready to potty train. That's great! But now, where do you start?

Explain to your toddler that going potty is a normal process of life, and everyone does it, even animals. Talk with them about the toilet, a special place where they can potty just like the big kids. Tell them how the potty works and let them try flushing themselves. Explain that they will be wearing underwear and not diapers. Find some educational and entertaining videos of their favorite characters learning to go potty. Be sure to involve other family members in the process and emphasize the importance of consistency during this process.

Make a special trip to the store and purchase new underwear with your toddler. Let them have a voice in what you get. The underwear will have much more significance if your toddler helped choose them.

Overalls, pants with lots of buttons, snaps or zips, tight or restrictive clothing and oversized shirts will all be obstacles to your child during this process. Put these kinds of clothes away for the time being.

Decide whether or not you're going to use pull-ups, training pants or regular underwear and try to stick with this decision so your child has consistency and isn't confused. Think about whether or not you want to use rewards or not. Figure out a strategy on how to handle potty issues when you're away from home.

If your child is in child care, ask your provider for their advice and make sure there aren't any hard and fast rules the center or caregiver has in place that may be an issue. Let them know that you're going to start and enlist their help with the process.

Praise your child for each successful trip to the potty and comfort them when accidents happen. Try to remain patient and calm when they do. Avoid using candy or other treats as reinforcement. Let them know that it will take a while to get the hang of using the potty, and encourage and praise each attempt they make. With consistency, encouragement and praise, they will soon be completely trained.

CHAPTER 5- THE PARENT PRESSURE AND THE PRESSURED CHILD

Parents naturally want their children to be the best, whether in academics or extra-curricular activities – or both! Young kids especially find happiness in pleasing their parents, and would do almost anything to garner their approval – from doing simple chores and creating pretty artwork, to accomplishing more ambitious feats like winning in sports or beauty pageants. But how far can we push our little ones without breaking their spirit or setting them up for disappointment?

Over competitive parents usually have many expectations from their children. They are more particular with good grades and performance than with how happy the child is going through schooling or joining an activity. For instance, some parents are still not satisfied when a child receives a B grade, expecting instead the perfect A. These parents see mistakes as unacceptable. Pointing fingers at who is to blame for the 'failure' of their child becomes their means to rectifying the situation, ignoring the possibility that there are other factors and variables at play. The worst scenario is when explanations are sought from the children, who may not always know why they performed below expectation.

Why the Pressure?

Here are several factors:

Family backgrounds

Continuing the family 'legacy' is important for most parents. For instance, if you come from a family of doctors, chances are, you will be expected to become one, too, regardless of your capacity or inclination. When one or both parents are achievers, they don't see any reason for their talents not to manifest themselves in their children.

Economic stress

Some average income earners force kids to excel beyond their abilities so they can avail of scholarship grants and minimize the cost of schooling in their budget.

Children owe it to them

Many parents think that the formula to their children's success is to provide them with everything. And since everything is given, there is no reason why they cannot excel. "If her child can do it, why can't mine?" Hearing parents boast about their kids' success causes other parents to fell envy and even self-doubt. Because they feel this way, parents then put more pressure on their kid.

There is a constructive side to instilling competitiveness: children tend to strive more and see for themselves what they are really capable of. Financial gain is another advantage. If your child performs well, he can be awarded scholarship grants and get good offers when he or she reaches high school or college levels. Prestige and popularity come with territory, too, because 'the ability of the child shines.' Though instilling competitiveness in our children has its benefits, experts agree that potential negative ramifications outweigh the positive.

The following are some of them:

Children become misguided.

When the pressure is too much, the child no longer sees knowledge and the acquisition of knowledge as goals. The grade has become the premium whether or not he or she learns anything that is of value to him or her. Also, the child becomes an unfriendly competitor.

Children can get easily frustrated.

Children under great pressure become very unhappy with one or two little mistakes. They may start blaming themselves for the slightest setback. They may start having sleepless nights. They will take every mistake of failure as the 'end of it all.' This kind of mindset – where personal worth is measured by grades, accolades, and other quantifiable achievements – can be detrimental to their self-perception.

Children become fearful.

With expectations set high, children may fear punishment from their parents every time they fall short. If children have difficulty in certain subjects or areas, they need support and guidance early on. However, since they are afraid of 'disappointing' their parents, they will not come out and say, "I am having a hard time understanding this." Nothing is resolved; no course of action is taken. This fear of failure also translates itself into children's unwillingness to take risks, to explore, or to try something new, thus stunting their development.

Children develop over-dependence on parents.

Children under tremendous pressure from their parents are usually unable to think for themselves. How happy they are with their achievements depends on how happy mom and dad are. They feel that their parents approve every move they make.

Children become socially isolated.

Constant bragging of parents about their children to others may not always be graciously received. This may even create a wall between the child being bragged about and others (friends, the school, community, even relatives). A child may develop either an unhealthy superiority or inferiority complex. The feeling of being better than everybody else, because a child was constantly drilled that he or she is can result in ostracism by peers. Similarly, feeling inferior to others may cause children to retreat into their shells.

Children measure self-worth with achievements.

When children hear their parents comparing them with others, it only translates to two messages: either "Mommy and Daddy love me because I am perfect," or "They say I'm not as good as the other kids." Thus, the need to succeed arises, but only to satisfy the desire to be accepted and be loved. Before anyone notices, what begins as self-doubt escalates into serious anxiety, which can lead to more serious problems, such as power struggles, eating disorders, and depression, even at a very young age.

Children need to know that they will be loved whether or not they receive any accolades. Preschoolers, in particular, should be guided more on mastering age-appropriate skills that will serve as their foundation for later learning, not on reaping awards or medals. The universal rights of children include not only the right to have food, shelter, and education, but the right to play as well. Therefore, it is important that parents find ways for children to also relax and have fun.

Be confident of your children's lead: Let them learn at their own pace, and be there to hold their hand when they need it. Keep in mind that accomplishments in infancy, toddler years, and preschool years do not necessarily predict a child's success in adulthood. Just as parents do best, love and accept your children for who they are. Allow them to be themselves and hit that road the way they see it. Each child is unique. Respect their ways of learning, growing, and thinking. Ultimately, children's true measure of greatness depends on the guidance and values their parents give them.

Are You a Pusher?

A 'yes' to more than three of these signs means you have to lighten up a bit!

-I feel extremely disappointed and worried when other children reach milestones earlier than my child does.

- During family gatherings, I urge my child to perform tricks for everyone whether he or she likes it or not.

- My child has the best voice in class, so he or she deserves to have the center spot in the special number.

- It doesn't bother me when other parents tell me about their kids. My child's accomplishments always outdo theirs.

- I always ask my child's scores in quizzes and exams, and then ask what his or her classmates' scores were.

- I always air out my complaints to my kid's teacher whenever I feel that my child didn't get the grade I think he deserves. I demand explanations and don't give up until I am satisfied with the answers.

CHAPTER 6- HOW TO TEACH YOUR KIDS VALUES AND GOOD BEHAVIOR

What can parents do now to prepare their kids in the right direction towards thinking for themselves and making good (or better) choices? Experience tells us that prudence can be realistically achieved not at seven (age of reason) but by the age of eighteen. Spanish educator David Isaacs, PhD suggests that parents lay the foundation for prudence by instilling four good habits during the first seven years of life. Namely: obedience, sincerity, order, and justice. He believes that these four habits are needed in the progressive development of other good habits within the next three phases: charity and fortitude (courage) in elementary level (8 to 12), faith and temperance (self-control) in adolescence (13-15), and hope and prudence (sound judgment) in young adulthood (16-18). Furthermore, those who have these virtues will naturally find happiness and human maturity, he concludes.

Obedience

A loving but firm parental authority exercised in each home prevents domestic chaos – clutter, sickness, hunger, shouting, violence, disrespect, and rebellion. Imagining chaos in infants and toddlers may seem tolerable, but when we project this in adolescents and grown-ups with a voice, a choice, and plenty of muscle... no one wants to end up the loser. Young children must learn to obey their parents' reasonable demands (not mere trivialities), but they also have to hear kind simple explanations to common rules, situations, and events. It is through a consistent, regular, and clear communication of the parents' pleasure or displeasure, approval or disapproval, happiness or sadness toward ideas, words, and/or actions that children begin to experience and understand the value system of their family. This value system will be validated, respected, or rejected in later life based on the methods used, attitudes absorbed, emotions attached, and information gathered from home, school, or elsewhere. Inconsistency will easily confuse inexperienced young minds, which have not yet learned the purpose of life.

Sincerity

Sincerity (telling the truth at the proper time and to the proper person) must be practiced at home. The children must imbibe it in the context of helping loved ones to improve (out of charity and justice). Children will likely be more confident in this type of home environment and prefer it to a contrary one. It will be difficult for the good and true to be embraced by those who grow up with lies and end up with bad habits (or vices) and muddled criteria. If they turn cynical and become individualistic – instead of accepting their vital role in the success of their own family, as well as the larger community – they delay their own chances for true and lasting happiness. And no parent consciously wants this to happen! Thus, it is critical for parents to expose their family members to reliable criteria and genuine good (not mere apparent good), so that they can encourage their children's potential abilities to know the truth and to love well. This is done using two of their more important, separate, but interlinked powers of the intellect and the will present in the soul of human beings, making us all accountable.

Order

The third habit of order provides the family, especially the young children, a sense of predictability and stability because procedures are followed and many things are done properly at their place and time. Nothing ruins a child's equilibrium more than disorder – in his caregiver, his schedule, his bed, and so on. Even parents need order to maintain their own well-being and sanity. Note that a lot of affection is more effective than reasoning in making sure family members get along well.

Justice

The young inherently value justice because of their natural demand for parental time and love, in competition with siblings, work, and other distractions (to a child's mind). They are ready to understand the importance of fairness in what is due them (or others) in ordinary circumstances. Adults are expected to apply rules and sanctions equitably lest children rebel and defy authority figures and rules. Children must get the message that life makes sense, rules make sense, and consequences make sense. They need to see things as they are over what they seem, and be able to choose a path that will lead them closer to universal values, or their 'true North's.'

How to Communicate with the Younger Generation

When parents speak with young children, alone or as a group, they must establish eye contact and/or hold them at close range, preferably at eye level, to maintain warm direct communication and rapport. It may be necessary for mothers and fathers to bend over, squat or kneel; or put down the newspaper, telephone, or cooking pan as well. In addition, a calm soothing tone of voice is preferred when giving instructions, and a firm serious one for reprimands. Smiling or laughing when children do wrong, and indifference or anger when they do right, goes against the proper formation of good criteria and good habits.

The goal is: a clear mind and a strong will. In small doses, at an early start, both mother and father can provide daily cues to their children about essential distinctions between fact and opinion, important and urgent, cause and effect, problem and solution, family and friend, male and female, public and private, right and wrong, rights and duties, life-threatening and life-saving, eternal and temporal... the list can go on. At times, it may be necessary to consult the right sources before making any decisions and following these through. Slowly, both parents and children understand their value system and communicate on the same level. Finally, a most important daily habit worth fostering until old age is self-reflection, answering the following three questions: What did I do right? What did I do wrong? And what can I do better?

What Parents Should Know and Teach About Lying

Honesty and dishonesty are learned in the home. Parents are often concerned when their child or adolescent lies.

The Less-Stressing Way of Educating Your Children

Young children often make up stories and tell tall tales. This is normal activity, because they enjoy hearing stories and making up stories for fun. These young children may blur the distinction between reality and fantasy. This is probably more a result of an active imagination than an attempt to deliberately lie about something.

An older child or adolescent may tell a lie to be self-serving, such as denying responsibility or to try to get out of a chore or task. Parents should respond to isolated instances of lying by talking with the youngster about the importance of truthfulness, honesty and trust.

Some adolescents discover that lying may be considered acceptable in certain situations, such as not telling a boyfriend or girlfriend the real reasons for breaking up with them because they don't want to hurt their feelings. Other adolescents may lie to protect their privacy or to help them feel psychologically separate and independent from their parents.

Parents are the most important role models for their children. When a child or adolescent lies, parents should take some time to have a serious talk and discuss the difference between make believe and reality, and lying and telling the truth. They should open an honest line of communication to find out exactly why the child chose to tell a lie, and to discuss alternatives to lying. A parent should lead by example and never lie, and when they are caught in a lie, express remorse and regret for making a conscious decision to tell a lie. Clear, understandable consequences for lying should be discussed with the child early on.

However, some forms of lying are cause for concern, and might indicate an underlying emotional problem. Some children who know the difference between truthfulness and lying tell elaborate stories which appear believable. Children or adolescents usually relate these stories with enthusiasm because they receive a lot of attention as they tell the lie.

Other children or adolescents who otherwise seem responsible fall into a pattern of repetitive lying. They often feel that lying is the easiest way to deal with the demands of parents, teachers and friends. These children are usually not trying to be bad or malicious, but the repetitive pattern of lying becomes a bad habit. A serious repetitive pattern of lying should be cause for concern. Consult a professional adolescent or child psychologist to find out whether help is needed.

CHAPTER 7- CREATING A SAFE WORLD FOR YOUR CHILDREN

Accidents in the home are the primary cause of death in U.S. children. By taking a few simple precautions, these injuries can be avoided, making your home safe for your child and the children who visit it.

In your kitchen, you should be sure to install safety latches on cabinets and drawers. This helps keep children out of the everyday household chemicals you use to clean your home and dishware with and also keeps them from grabbing sharp objects like scissors or knives from inside the drawers. Use the back burners when cooking on the stovetop and keep the handles of your pots and pans turned out of a curious child's reach while cooking.

Safety latches should be installed on cabinets and drawers in your bathrooms, as well, to keep them out of unsafe household cleaning products and medicines. Be sure to unplug any electrical appliances, such as blow dryers or curling irons, directly after use, and put them out of a child's reach. Teach children early on that electricity and water do not mix and that no electrical appliances of any kind should ever be immersed in or placed under running water. Toilet locks should also be used in homes that have small children to keep lids down. Young children are 'top heavy' and can easily fall into a toilet if they lean in to play in it. Since a young child can drown in less than an inch of water, it is imperative to closely supervise them in the bathroom at all times.

Around your house, be sure to secure furniture, such as bookshelves and heavy furniture that could tip easily, to the wall using brackets. Use doorknob covers to keep children out of rooms with potential hazards and to keep them from leaving the house unsupervised. Make sure your window blinds do not have looped cords on them, as they can present a strangulation hazard to a young child. And always cover your electrical outlets with protective covers to keep small fingers from them and small objects from being inserted into them.

Check your house over carefully for other potential hazards and address them immediately. With these precautions and some common sense, your household will be your child's haven.

Armoring Your Child with Self-Esteem

As parents, we fear the worst for our children. We see an imperfect world, where strangers and circumstances can discourage, frighten, harm, or endanger our little ones. But kids need not be plagued with thoughts of a dangerous world, and parents shouldn't feel the need to create a protective bubble around them. The best defense is to empower kids with a boost of confidence and how-to-deal skills when facing possible dangers.

Self-esteem is the collection of beliefs or feelings that we have about ourselves, or our 'self-perceptions.' How we define ourselves influences our motivations, attitudes, and behaviors, and affects our emotional judgment. Self-esteem includes other qualities, such as self-confidence, pride, independence, self-reliance, and self-respect. Experts say we develop our self-esteem during childhood, and it constantly evolves as we are shaped by the different social interactions and experiences we go through. Enhancing a child's self-esteem is the first step to ensuring his or her right to personal safety. Keeping children away from physical harm is only secondary. Programs have been developed to teach children self-protective skills, and families recognize and respond to potentially unsafe situations. Children who are conscious of their self-worth feel good about themselves, pulling out all the stops to any sign of threat or danger. Moreover, self-esteem develops the same positive communication skills and attitudes, which children could pass on to the next generation.

A child's self-esteem is based on a positive relationship with parents and eventually teachers. Parents can foster that can-do attitude in their children with a "Wow!" or a "That's great!" every time they accomplish a feat. These positive comments form the children's first concept of success, which ultimately leads to a healthy self-perception. But praise and positive reinforcement alone will not make children feel better automatically. Providing them with lots of love, care, and understanding is equally significant. Children who are happy and confident may still experience low self-esteem because they do not feel loved. Likewise, children who are loved and pampered at home may still feel inadequate and incompetent, thus ending up with low self-esteem. Hence, a balance of both should be present. Delivering positive messages and engaging in constructive communication lead to a healthy self-perception.

Try these time-tested tips to enhance your child's can-do attitude.

1. Limit the "Don'ts" to the barest minimum. State your requests positively. Too many negative words in your sentences will only lead to a child's self-doubt.

2. Let kids complete their sentences. Avoid interruptions, as these disrupt their train of thought or make them forget what they're saying. Otherwise, they'll feel as if their ideas are insignificant and not worth listening to.

3. Establish eye contact. Be a good model of conversation by giving kids your full attention. This communicates that you are interested in what they are saying, and that you are stressing a noteworthy idea, as well.

4. Take turns in the conversation. Agree on who speaks first, and who speaks next. It is important for parents to encourage kids to verbalize their ideas and feelings, but to also wait for the go signal to speak. Children should be able to understand that if people talk all at the same time, they will end up understanding nothing.

5. Keep a calm, uncritical, and non-irritable manner when explaining. Keep your "speech" concise. Use language that kids will easily understand, explaining to them what they need to do, and why they should or should not do it. Speaking in a calm tone also keeps panic from rising within them.

6. Criticisms should still be present. We should also take notice of shortcomings or misbehavior as we see it or learn about it. Explain

why an action is not acceptable, and allow kids to think of ways to avoid doing it again.

Smart Thinking

Facing challenges and rising from them is a way to help strengthen a child's spirit. Though parents would prefer to totally shield their children from threats and hardship, doing so would cause as much damage. And let's face it: Adversity is inevitable. But training our children to become prudent and intelligent thinkers is a surefire way to protect them from possible harm. An effective method to hone children's thinking skills is to practice what if scenarios with them.

Children need to feel as if they have discovered why they should avoid potentially dangerous circumstances. Parents can engage in a dialogue with their kids. It's important to let them think for themselves, to foster their problem-solving skills. Parents shouldn't dictate the solution, but rather, allow kids to answer first, and then guide them unhurriedly to every possible avenue. We can't control what our children do every minute. But we can help them think, early in their lives, about what is and what is not safe, so we can trust them to take responsibility for their actions and to make safe decisions now and as they mature. Here are some possible danger scenarios, plus pre-emptive tips:

What You Can Do

Teach kids to pay attention to their instincts. Parents should tell their kids to listen to that voice in their heads; if they don't feel safe or they feel it's not right, they shouldn't go through with it. We need to give children safety nets of people they can go to if they need help, such as uniformed law-enforcement or security officers, a store salesperson with a nametag, the person in an information booth at a mall or other public venue, or a mother with children. Next, describe the proper way to handle a stranger.

A common ploy for abduction attempts are for strangers to pretend that they are friends of the child's parents, and that the parents – who are either sick or injured – asked them to pick the child up on their behalf. To help children deal with this particular situation, let them run the scenario in their heads, and then ask them the following questions:

- What do you do when a person you don't know says mommy or daddy asked him or her to pick you up from school, and that you should hop into the car?

- Do you run to your teacher, the principal, or the security guard?

- What do you do if the stranger grabs you?

- What do you think is the safest thing to do while waiting for mommy or daddy after school?

- Do you stay with your teacher in the classroom or the principal's office?

Should a stranger grab your kids, children should be taught to run for help and scream, kick, make a loud noise and keep yelling something like "You're not my mother!" or "You're not my father!" More importantly, teach your child from a very young age why he or she should never go anywhere with any adult, without your permission, whether that person is a stranger or a friend.

Bully Alert

Bullies pick on kids who are often alone, shy, quiet, and look like they can't stand up for themselves. Kids become victims of bullies because they have a very poor self-concept, believing their own dignity and self-worth are unimportant. What's worse is that most bullied kids are too afraid to tell their parents – either because they are scared their parents will think they're weak, or because they think their parents won't do much to rectify the situation.

What You Can Do

To help kids deal with bullying and prevent them from becoming bully victims, teach them the lesson of reciprocity. Help them realize that relationships are reciprocal, and that they should treat others as they wish to be treated. They will come to realize that people act as they do for many different reasons. Asking children questions that pay attention to their and other people's feelings also helps.

These questions include:

- Why do you think bullies need to pick on others?

- Do you have another reason?

- What do you think a bully is feeling or thinking?

- How would you feel if a kid bullies you?

- What can you do or say if you're being bullied? By fostering a climate of empathy at home, children learn the value of self-worth for themselves and for others.

According to child experts, you should let your child know that he or she has a right to insist that others treat him or her with respect and dignity. They are not to tolerate cruelty of any form, whether in real life, in the form of nasty jokes on sitcoms, or in other forms of entertainment. Stranger Danger "Don't talk to strangers" is not necessarily the key. We cannot expect our kids to do this if we adults break this rule every time – in the grocery store, waiting in line at the movie house, or even in school.

Children should know that most adults they encounter are basically good people. Often, these "strangers" are actually people who can help kids in case of emergencies.

How to Create a Positive Learning Environment

It has been shown many times over in research studies that a parent who is involved in their child's education has a positive impact. It's reflected in improved grades and test scores, strong attendance, a higher rate of homework completion, higher graduation rates, improved attitudes and behaviors in the child, as well as the child being more likely to become involved in positive extra-curricular activities. Send out the message early in your child's education that your home is an involved and active supporter of their learning.

Probably the most important element of a positive learning environment at home is structure. But what is too little or too much? If we're too lenient or expect too little, your child may become disorganized or unmotivated. If we're too rigid and strict, it can cause undue pressure or cause your child to feel unable to deliver on your expectations.

So what's the best way to meet in the middle and create a positive learning environment for your child at home?

Help your child develop a work area where they can study and focus without being interrupted. Children usually do better when they have a private study area away from interruption. If your child prefers doing their work at the kitchen table, make sure other family members understand the kitchen is off-limits during study time. Make sure your child has plenty of supplies and reference materials available and that the area has plenty of light. Regardless of its location, ensure the area is quiet and that your child can study and work uninterrupted.

Agree on a regular time for studying. To help your child make homework a habit, schedule a set time each day for homework. Perhaps breaking study time up into smaller increments would work better for your child than one solid period. Work with your child to find out what works best for them. In addition, be sure your child has a sufficient break between the time they arrive home from school and the time they sit down to work, in order to 'decompress' from their school day.

Help your child develop a method of keeping track of homework assignments. This can be a difficult chore for some students. Developing a successful way of keeping track of assignments, then scratching them off as completed, helps them develop a productive method for accomplishing tasks later in life.

Develop a positive line of communication with your child's teacher. Teachers are usually very willing and excited to work with an involved parent to help the child's overall success in school. Whether they're notes sent back and forth in your child's backpack or an e-mail correspondence, make sure your teacher knows your open for suggestions as to how to better assist them in the homework and study process at home.

CHAPTER 8- A CHILD'S RIGHT TO PLAY

For children, play is naturally enjoyable. And since it is their active engagement in things that interest them, play should be child-led, or at least child-inspired, for it to remain relevant and meaningful to them. Children at play are happily lost in themselves; they are in their own realm of wonder, exploration, and adventure, pulling parents in at times with a frequent "Let's play, mom!" as an open invitation into that world. As early as infancy, children immerse themselves in play activities with the purpose of making sense of the world around them.

Play gives children the opportunity to learn and experience things themselves, which is vital for their development. Although peek-a-boo games seem pointless to adults, tots are awed by the surprise that awaits them as they see the suddenly emerging faces of people they love.

Stages of Play

During toddlerhood, children experience a motor-growth spurt that equips them to solitarily fiddle with anything they can get their hands on – be it a construction toy or the box from where it came. Toddlers also love breaking into song, wiggling and jiggling to tunes, and imitating finger plays they are commonly exposed to. Preschoolers begin extending their play to involve others, whether they bring others in at any stage of their game or they plan their game and its players' way ahead. Their physical and motor skills allow them to widen their lay arena, from dramatic play to table games to outdoor pursuits. School-age children start appreciating organized play – such as innovated songs and rhymes, games with rules, relays and other physical activities, sports and projects that they can accomplish over a certain time frame.

The Advantages of Playing

Why the big fuss about playing? Play benefits the child in ways that might be a tad difficult for adults to imagine.

1. Play brings pure and utter joy. A toddler who jumps into an empty box and runs around the house 'driving a car' shows the sheer happiness that play brings him or her. When children are asked what they did in school and they answer 'play,' it is a clear sign that these kids remember a feeling of genuine joy that is captured in this four-letter word.

2. Play fosters socio-emotional learning. What does a ten-month-old baby who shrieks at the sight of her stuffed toy have in common with a ten-year-old boy who plays basketball with his

friends? They both deal with their confidence as they choose to embark on their play activities. At the same time, they are displaying their independence in the decisions that they make. These two children are also internalizing social rules in their respective play situations: the baby waits patiently for her stuffed toy to appear, while the school-age child has to contend with an impending loss in a ball game.

3. Play hones physical and motor development. Play often involves the use of the senses, the body, and the extremities. When children play, they exercise their bodies for physical strength, fluidity of movement, balance and coordination. Perceptual-motor ability, or the capacity to coordinate what you perceive with how you move, is an essential skill that preschoolers need to develop. A three-year-old who is engrossed in digging, scooping, and pouring sand into a container must match his or her perception of the space in front of him or her with actual hand movements, so that he or she can successfully fulfill the motor activity.

4. Play facilitates cognitive learning. Play is vital to the intellectual development of a child. We live in a symbolic world in which people need to decode words, actions, and numbers. For young children, symbols do not naturally mean anything because they are just arbitrary representations of actual objects. The role of play is for the child to understand better cognitive concepts in ways that are enjoyable, real, concrete, and meaningful to them. For instance, through play, a child is able to comprehend that the equation 3 + 2 = 5 means 'putting together' his toy cars by lining them up in his makeshift parking lot. When he combines 2 triangles to make a square during block play, or writes down his score is a bowling game, the child is displaying what he knows about shapes and numbers. Through play, the child is constructing his or her worldview by constantly working and reworking his understanding of concepts.

5. Play enhances language development. Toddlers who are still grappling with words need to be immersed in oral language so they can imitate what they hear. They benefit from songs and rhymes that provide the basis for understanding how language works. When these tots are playing with toys, adults model to them how language is used to label objects or describe an event. At play, preschoolers use language to interact, communicate ideas, and likewise learn from dialogues with more mature members of society.

6. Play encourages creativity. Barney the dinosaur was right about using imagination to make things happen. A lump of Play-Doh suddenly turns into spaghetti with meat sauce and cheese; a small towel transforms into a cape that completes a superhero's wardrobe; and a tin can serves as a drum that accompanies an aspiring rock artist. Play opens an entire avenue for children to express themselves, show what they know and how they feel, and to create their own masterpieces.

7. Play provides bonding opportunities. Play is an important factor in child development. It provides for interaction, experimentation, and moral development. Here are some ways by which parents can encourage and support their children's playtime. Let your child be the player-leader. Allow them to initiate activities, set their own theme, and choose the parameters where the play will take place. Play becomes a venue for children to express their feelings and be in control.

- Help them help themselves. When your 5-year-old asks for help, say, figuring out how to piece a puzzle together, stop yourself from coming to her rescue and first ask your child questions that allow him or her to help himself or herself. Say, "Where do you think this piece should go?" Afterward, commend his or her success.

- Play attention. Once you make a commitment to play with your child, watch for the following signals: Does he or she want you to actively play a part in the activity? Does he or she need encouragement? Is he or she tired or hungry? Does he or she need to take a break?

- Have a play plan. If you seem to have little time for playing with your child, consider using self-care chores to have fun with him or her. Also, get support from other people in your household, like older siblings, household help, or the child's grandparents, so that they understand why play is important and how they should continue to encourage it.

How to Handle Tantrums

Even the best-behaved toddler has an occasional temper tantrum. A tantrum can range from whining and crying to screaming, kicking, hitting, and breath holding. They are equally common in boys and girls and usually occur from age 1 to age 3. Some children may experience regular tantrums, whereas for other children, tantrums may be rare. Some kids are more prone to throwing a temper tantrum than others.

Toddlers are trying to master the world, and when they aren't able to accomplish a task, they often use one of the only tools at their disposal for venting frustration - a tantrum. There are several basic causes of tantrums that are familiar to parents everywhere: The child is seeking attention, or is tired, hungry, or uncomfortable. In addition, tantrums are often the result of children's frustration with the world. Frustration is an unavoidable part of kids' lives as they learn how people, objects, and their own bodies work.

Tantrums are common during the second year of life, a time when children are acquiring language. Toddlers generally understand more than they can express. As language skills improve, tantrums tend to decrease.

Keep off-limits objects out of sight and out of reach, which will make struggles less likely to develop over them. Distract your child. Take advantage of your little one's short attention span by offering a replacement for the coveted object or beginning a new activity to replace the frustrating or forbidden one. And choose your battles: consider the request carefully when your child wants something. Is it outrageous? Maybe it isn't. Accommodate, when possible, to avoid an outburst.

Make sure your child isn't acting up simply because he or she isn't getting enough attention. To a child, negative attention (a parent's response to a tantrum) is better than no attention at all. Try to establish a habit of catching your child being good ("time in"), which means rewarding your little one with attention and praise for positive behavior. This will teach them that acting appropriately makes mommy and daddy happy and proud, and they'll be anxious to do it again and again.

Taming the Biting Toddler

The majority of toddlers engage in some biting between their first and third birthdays. Probably the most common reason is that it is one of the few ways of communicating that are effective for them, before verbal skills are developed. However, not all children bite. Some choose other forms of communication, such as grabbing, shoving, or punching.

Another reason toddlers bite is to express frustration, a feeling which is very common with toddlers, because both their communication skills and their motor skills are so limited.

To a young toddler it can be funny to see mommy suddenly bolt upright or for a playmate to start crying. Toddlers may also bite because they're teething or because they put everything in their mouths anyway, so why not someone's arm? It could even be something as simple as hunger.

But how do you teach your child not to bite? Make it perfectly clear that the biting is hurtful and wrong, and point out to your child how much pain their biting has caused. Express that biting is wrong and unacceptable, and that either mommy or daddy likes it.

If you discover that your child is biting out of frustration, try giving them an alternative way to express to people that they are having a difficult time. Though language is a difficult task at this age, most toddlers can be taught words that are appropriate for such a situation. For instance, "You need to tell mommy or daddy that you need help and not bite us," or "Show mommy what you need, but don't bite. You'll hurt her if you bite, and I know you don't want to hurt mommy, do you?"

Experts agree that parents should try not to give biting so much attention that it becomes an attention-getter. This is true of all behavior that you don't want to see repeated. Firmly tell the child again that there is no biting allowed, that it is wrong, and that it hurts people.

Raising Gender-Sensitive Children

We find it normal when boys mess around with plastic popguns and girls play with floral patterned tea sets. But if they trade toys, most of us are overcome with uneasiness, shock, or even anger. Experts say that kids grow into well-rounded adults if their parents allow them to explore all possibilities – and this includes stripping them of gender biases. Therefore, seeing your baby girl play with toy cars and Junior play with Barbie Dolls shouldn't be viewed as a threat, but as an avenue for children to reach their full potential.

Children begin to form their own concept of gender identity – or the sense of being a boy or a girl – by age one. Some say gender identity is biologically determined. Most psychologists, however, believe that gender identity is determined by environmental factors, particularly in the way parents, relatives, and peers treat children. Once a child's gender identity is established, "gender stability" takes place – which is when children develop gender-typical behaviors. Though physically different, both girls and boys should be given equal opportunities to develop their potentials to the fullest. Doing so boosts their self-image and emotional stability. By removing gender stereotypes, you allow your children to explore and develop latent gifts and talents that could otherwise be left untapped.

It is possible to raise children who are not 'sexist' in their points of view, who have respect for both males and females. Positive parent and teacher child interactions are crucial in forming bias-free outlooks, attitudes, and actions in children. For instance, encourage both boys and girls to keep their rooms clean, fold their own clothes, and put their shoes in place. Just because a woman usually cleans up the mess, it doesn't mean that only females perform these chores. Also, mom and dad should switch household chores once in a while. Dad can do the cooking or iron the clothes, while mom takes out the trash or washes the car. Allow both girls and boys to express their emotions. A boy has as much right to break out in tears as a girl has to show assertive behavior in venting her frustration. In addition, boys should be taught to be nurturing and compassionate, while praise and courage should be instilled in girls.

Chapter 9- How to Raise Healthy Children

Recent studies have shown that not only do children like to sit down at the dinner table and eat a meal with their parents, but they also are more likely to eat a well-balanced, nutritious meal when they do. But with the hectic lives we seem to lead these days, getting the family all together in the same place at the same time can be a difficult chore. Between work schedules, after-school activities, errands, and the like, it seems we have less and less time. But with a few simple ideas and some planning, meal time can be an enjoyable and treasured family time.

Designate no less than one night per week to have a sit-down meal with your family. Sunday nights are usually a good choice for this, because you have more time to relax and the weekend chores have been completed.

Involve your children in the meal planning and preparation. This gives them a strong sense of self and the foundation for a lifetime of healthy meal planning and preparation.

Make sure the television is off and make it a rule that all phone calls go to voice mail or the answering machine during the meal. Take this time to visit with one another and enjoy one another's company. This is a great time to reconnect and find out what events happened this week. Take your time eating, and teach your children how to do the same in the process. Eating slowly is a healthy habit. Don't jump up and start clearing dishes and putting things away until everyone is done eating and talking.

On those days that you can't sit down as a family, try to make a habit of sitting down and chatting with your child while they are eating, instead of rushing around catching up on the chores. This shows them that you're interested, and that you care and want to be an involved and important part of their everyday life.

The Importance of Routine

Regular schedules provide the day with a structure that orders a young child's world. Although predictability can be tiresome for adults, children thrive on repetition and routine. Schedules begin from the first days of life. Babies, especially, need regular sleep and meal programs and even routines leading up to those activities.

As they get older, when a child knows what is going to happen and who is going to be there, it allows them to think and feel more independently, and feel more safe and secure. A disrupted routine can set a child off and cause them to feel insecure and irritable.

Dinner time is a great place to start setting a routine. Sitting together at the dinner table gives children the opportunity to share their day and talk about their feelings. This is also a great time to include some responsibility in your child's routine, such as helping to set or clear the table.

And regardless of how exhausted you or your children may be, don't be tempted to skip winding down from the day. This is part of a nighttime ritual and allows both child and parent to decompress after a busy day. It also helps bedtime go more smoothly. This is usually the time of day when parent and child can spend some quality time together, so fight the urge to start the laundry or do the dishes until after the child has gone to bed. If this isn't possible, consider trading off these duties with your spouse each night to ensure your child has quality time with each parent on a regular basis. Take the time to find out what wind-down strategy works best for your child. Some children are actually energized instead of relaxed by a warm bath, so if that's the case with your child, bath time should be saved for a different time of day. Whatever routine you settle on, make it quiet, relaxing, and tranquil for everyone.

And though routines are essential, there should be some room to be flexible as well. You might be out late at night on a family outing, or have unexpected company show up that may result in a skipped meal or nap in the car while running errands in the evening. In these instances, it's important for you to keep your cool. If you express frustration or anger about the disruption of the routine, your child will as well. Prepare children for such unexpected events and show them that though it can happen from time to time, the routine will return the next day.

Taking Out the Fuss in Eating

Toddlers can be fussy eaters who refuse to try a new food at least half of the time. Approximately half of all toddlers fit this description, so it is no wonder that food issues are a source of stress for parents.

Establishing healthy eating patterns is important to avoid problems such as obesity and eating disorders later in life. Various strategies can help your child accept a wider range of foods. It may be necessary to offer a food to your child as many as 10 different times before they choose to eat it. The problem is, many parents get frustrated and give up before the fourth or fifth try.

Try to make foods fun. Colorful foods like carrot sticks, raisins, apples, grapes, cheese sticks and crackers can all be fun and healthy choices for your growing toddler. Explain to them that eating good food is important so they'll grow big and strong, and how it will help them run faster and play longer.

Children learn behaviors from their parents. If you restrict yourself to a narrow range of foods, your child will take notice and mimic your caution. Don't limit your child's food variety to only those foods you prefer. It may be that your child's tastes are different from yours, and perhaps you are simply serving them foods they don't happen to like. Try to set a good example and try a variety of foods in front of your child. It could motivate them to do the same.

If your child seems healthy and energetic, then they are eating enough. If you are still concerned, keep an eye on how much food they actually eat over the course of a day. Children tend to graze constantly, rather than restrict their eating to three meals per day like adults. You may be surprised how those little handfuls and snacks add up. For further reassurance, check your child's growth and weight charts, or check with your child's pediatrician.

Try not to worry and remember that unless a child is ill, they will eat. Children are very good at judging their hunger and fullness signals. Try to stay relaxed about mealtime and offer your child a wide variety of foods, and most importantly, remember to set a good example by trying a wide variety of foods yourself. You may discover you and your toddler share a new found favorite food!

ABOUT THE AUTHOR

Ruth Hill is a child psychologist at a local children's hospital in Mississippi. She has handled cases ranging in severity – from domestic abuse to trauma cases.

Ruth, herself, grew up in an abusive home. Daughter of a drunkard of a father, her mother fled when she was still a youngster. She is "experience is the best teacher" personified.

Today, Ruth has a happy home with a loving husband and an amazing child.

Lightning Source UK Ltd.
Milton Keynes UK
UKOW01f1219070917
308750UK00006B/938/P